ROOM
by ROOM Quilts

LEISURE ARTS, INC.
Little Rock, Arkansas

EDITORIAL STAFF
Editor-in-Chief: Susan White Sullivan
Quilt and Craft Publications Director:
  Cheryl Johnson
Special Projects Director: Susan Frantz Wiles
Senior Prepress Director: Mark Hawkins
Art Publications Director: Rhonda Shelby
Imaging Technician: Stephanie Johnson
Prepress Technician: Janie Marie Wright
Photography Manager: Katherine Laughlin
Contributing Photographers: Ken West
Contributing Photo Stylists: Sondra Daniel
Publishing Systems Administrator:
Becky Riddle
Mac Information Technology Specialist:
Robert Young

BUSINESS STAFF
President and Chief Executive Officer:
  Rick Barton
Vice President of Sales: Mike Behar
Director of Finance and Administration:
  Laticia Mull Dittrich
National Sales Director: Martha Adams
Creative Services: Chaska Lucas
Information Technology Director: Hermine Linz
Controller: Francis Caple
Vice President, Operations: Jim Dittrich
Retail Customer Service Manager: Stan Raynor
Print Production Manager: Fred F. Pruss

Library of Congress Control Number: 2011940920

ISBN-13: 978-1-60900-414-9

Barbara Cherniwchan

"My mom was an art teacher and I started to craft as soon as I was able to hold a crayon. She taught me and my two sisters every craft under the sun which eventually led me to quilting."

Barbara retired from the practice of law in order to be at home with her growing family. As the kids got older, Barbara began a new career in quilting with an online quilt shop, then two brick and mortar stores, then a wholesale pattern partnership, then designing quilt patterns. This is her first book. She now works with a number of fabric designers from Moda to create patterns inspired by the fabric they design. Check out more designs by Barbara at www.coachhousedesigns.com. Barbara lives in Chilliwack, British Columbia with her husband and four children.

Thank you to my friend Marcia Boulanger for helping me piece and my daughters, Danielle and Holly, for making appliqué shapes. I could not have finished in time without you.

Thank you also to Linda and Rhonda of Quilted Cats Hideway for thier fabulous machine quilting and putting up with my deadlines.

Table of Contents

Appliqué Supplies

Freezer Paper

I use white freezer paper, which you can purchase at your local grocery store, for tracing and cutting out templates. Freezer paper is matte finish on one side and shiny on the other. Trace onto the matte size and press the shiny side down to temporarily adhere it to your fabric. A freezer paper template can be re-used several times before it needs replacing.

Thread and Hand Needles

I use YLI Silk Thread for hand-appliqué. The fine thread is barely visible. Choose a neutral color which blends well with all your appliqué pieces. I like to use Jeanna Kimball's Foxglove Cottage Size 11 Straw Needles with the silk thread.

Water Soluble Liquid Basting Glue

I use Roxanne™ Glue-Baste-It to make my applique shapes for hand and machine appliqué. It is water soluble and has a fine tip which easily controls the flow of the glue. If you like this appliqué method, invest in a big bottle.

Basting Spray

I also use 505® Spray and Fix to baste large appliqué shapes for Rough Edge Appliqué. Place the shape in a cardboard box lid with the wrong side facing up. Spray the back of the shape and it is ready to be placed on the quilt top. The shape can be lifted and moved to another place but be careful not to pull too hard at the edge of the shape when lifting it up or it will fray.

Appliqué Techniques

Appliqué Templates

All appliqué templates are found in the center pull-out section.

Rough Edge Appliqué

1. Trace the appliqué shapes onto the matte side of freezer paper. Cut the traced shapes out slightly larger than the drawn lines.
2. Refer to the pattern instructions to determine which shapes are to be cut from which fabrics.
3. Using an iron, press the template, shiny side down, onto the right side of the appropriate fabric.
4. Cut out along the drawn lines of the template, through the paper and fabric.
5. Repeat until all the shapes are cut out.
6. Refer to the Appliqué Layout Diagram included with the pattern instructions to place the pieces. Refer also to the pattern instructions to determine the order in which the appliqué pieces should be attached.
7. Tack the appliqué pieces to the background with Water Soluble Liquid Basting Glue about ¼" in from the outer edges of the pieces or you can spray the back of the pieces with 505 Basting Spray which will keep them in place long enough to sew them down. Pin the center of the larger shapes to make sure they lie flat.
8. Use a smaller stitch setting on your machine to attach the pieces to the quilt top and sew ⅛" in from the edges of the shapes. Once washed, the pieces will have a slightly rough edge to them.

Machine Appliqué

1. Using the templates provided, trace the appliqué shapes onto the matte side of freezer paper. Cut out along the drawn line.
2. Using an iron, press the template, shiny side down, onto the right side of the appropriate fabric. Cut the fabric ⅛" to ¼" larger than the paper template as shown in Fig. 1.

Fig. 1

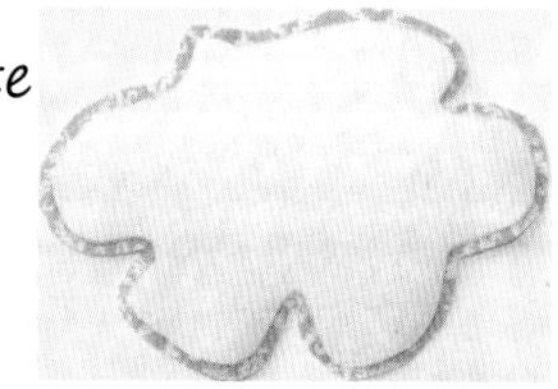

3. Turn the template over so that the wrong side of the fabric is facing up. If necessary, snip the inside curves to within 1 or 2 threads of the template so that the fabric can be folded to the back along the edge of the template.

Fig. 2

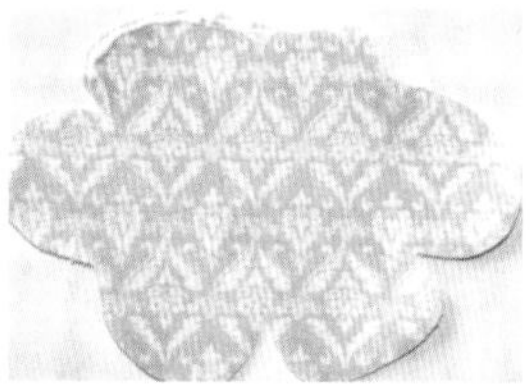

4. Apply a thin line of water soluble liquid basting glue along the overhanging edge (Fig. 2) and using your fingers, an awl or the tip of a seam ripper, press the overhanging edge to the back of the shape using the template edge as a guide as shown in Fig. 3.

Fig. 3

5. Remove the freezer paper and re-use the template if necessary. If you are making several of the same shape, like the petals for Holly's Quilt in Room 3, make multiple copies of the same template to allow you to work on several

shapes at once. (If the basting glue is visible on the front of the appliqué shapes, it can be dabbed off with a damp cloth after they are sewn to the backgrounds)

6. Refer to the Appliqué Layout Diagram included with the pattern instructions to place the pieces. Refer also to the pattern instructions to determine the order in which the appliqué pieces should be attached.

7. Apply small dots of the liquid basting glue about ¼" in from the edge on the wrong side of the appliqué shapes. Gently press the shapes to the background to secure them in place.

8. Sew the shapes to the background using an appliqué stitch on your machine such as a blanket or satin stitch. I used a blanket stitch when making the quilts shown in this book. (see "Machine Blanket Stitch" under General Instructions on page 60)

Hand Appliqué

1. Repeat steps 1 – 7 under Machine Appliqué to prepare the appliqué shapes.

2. Sew the shapes to the background using a blind stitch. Use YLI Silk Thread and a straw needle and your stitches will be nearly invisible. (see "Blind Stitch" under General Instructions on page 64)

Gathered Circles Appliqué

1. Using the circle templates provided, trace the circles onto regular paper following the dotted line. Cut out the paper templates along this line and label them with the letter "A".

2. Trace the template again, this time following along the solid line. Cut out the paper template along this line and label them with the letter "B".

3. Use a glue stick to paste the templates to a light cardboard or cereal box and cut out the templates again.

4. Use the "A" template to trace the circle shape onto the wrong side of the appropriate fabric. Cut out along the drawn line.

5. Thread a hand needle with sturdy thread and knot the end. With the right side of the fabric circle facing up, use a basting stitch to sew along the outer edge of the circle about ⅛" in from the outer edge as shown in Fig. 4. When you get back to where you started, place the "B" template in the center of the back of the fabric circle and gather the outer edge, pulling the gathering tight around the template. Secure the gathering with 2 anchor stitches as shown in Fig. 5.

6. Press the circle and gently remove the template by bending the template slightly. Re-press after removing the template to maintain the shape.

7. Sew the shapes to the background using an appliqué stitch on your machine such as a blanket or satin stitch. I used a blanket stitch when making the quilts shown in this book. (see "Machine Blanket Stitch" under General Instructions on page 60)

Fig. 4

Fig. 5

Family Room
Lily's Throw

Fabric Requirements

Finished Quilt Size: 72" square
Finished Block Size: 16" square
Yardage is based on
43"/44" wide fabric

 Fabric 1 – 1⅞ yds for Border, Block B, Binding and Appliqué

 Fabric 2 – 1¾ yds for Blocks A & B

 Fabric 3 – ¼ yd for Block A

 Fabric 4 – 1 yd for Appliqué

 Fabric 5 – ¾ yd for Block B

 Fabric 6 – ⅛ yd for Appliqué

 Fabric 7 – ¾ yd for Block A

 Fabric 8 – 1⅝ yds for Blocks A & B

You will also need:
Backing Fabric – 4½ yds
80" square batting
Freezer Paper
Water Soluble Liquid Basting Glue

Cutting for Block A (8)

Follow **Rotary Cutting**, page 58, to cut pieces. Cut all strips from the selvage-to-selvage width of fabric. All measurements include ¼" seam allowances.

From Fabric 7:

Cut 2—8½" strips
 Sub-cut 8—8½" squares
Cut 2—2½" strips
 Sub-cut 32—2½" squares

From Fabric 2:

Cut 23—1½" strips
 Sub-cut 192—1½" x 2½" rectangles (set 96 aside for Block B)
 128—1½" x 3½" rectangles (set 64 aside for Block B)
Cut 2—2½" strips
 Sub-cut 32—2½" squares
Cut 5—2⅞" strips
 Sub-cut 64—2⅞" squares (set 32 aside for Block B)

From Fabric 3:

Cut 2—2½" strips
 Sub-cut 32—2½" squares

From Fabric 8:

Cut 5—2⅞" strips
 Sub-cut 64—2⅞" squares (set 32 aside for Block B)
Cut 11—2½" strips
 Sub-cut 128—2½" x 3½" rectangles (set aside 64 for Block B)
Cut 4—1½" strips
 Sub-cut 32—1½" x 4½" rectangles

Building Block A

Follow **Machine Piecing** and **Pressing**, pages 58 & 60, to assemble quilt top. Measure your work as you go to ensure that it matches the measurements provided and adjust your seam allowances as needed.

1. Block A is made up of 3 sections: the Center 8½" block, the Flower Buds in the corners,

   and the Vines between the Buds,

2. To build the Flower Buds, draw a diagonal line on the wrong side of the 2⅞" Fabric 8 squares. Place the Fabric 8 squares on top of 2⅞" Fabric 2 squares.

3. Using the diagonal line as a guide, sew a scant ¼" seam on either side of the line. Cut along the drawn line and press the squares open You should have 64 "leaf" squares measuring 2½" square. Trim if necessary.

4. Attach a 2½" Fabric 3 square to the top of 32 leaf squares, a 2½" Fabric 2 square to the bottom of the 32 remaining leaf squares as shown in paragraph 1 and then join the Flower Buds sections together.

5. To build the Vines Section, attach a 1½" x 2½" Fabric 2 rectangle to the bottom edge of 64 - 2½" x 3½" Fabric 8 rectangles. Set aside.

6. Attach a 1½" x 2½" Fabric 2 rectangles to the top edge of 32—2½" Fabric 7 squares. Next attach a 1½" x 3½" Fabric 2 rectangle to either side of the squares. Then attach a 1½" x 4½" Fabric 8 rectangle on the top edge.

7. Attach a paragraph 6 unit on either side of the paragraph 7 units to complete the Vines Sections.

8. Attach a Vines Section to the top and bottom edge of the 8½" Fabric 7 squares

9. Attach a Flower Buds Section on either end of the remaining Vines Sections so that the pink buds are pointing away from the Center Section. Attach to the sides of the Block A.

Cutting for Block B (8)

From Fabric 5:

Cut 2—8½" strips
 Sub-cut 8—8½" squares
Cut 2—2½" strips
 Sub-cut 32—2½" squares

From Fabric 2:

Cut 2—2½" strips
 Sub-cut 32—2½" squares

From Fabric 1:

Cut 2—2½" strips
 Sub-cut 32—2½" squares

From Fabric 8:

Cut 4—1½" strips
 Sub-cut 32—1½" x 4½" rectangles

Building Block B

Block B is constructed the same way as Block A except the 2½" Fabric 3 squares in the Buds Sections are replaced with 2½" Fabric 1 squares, the 2½" Fabric 7 squares in the Vines Section are replaced with 2½" Fabric 5 squares and the Center Section is a 8½" Fabric 5 square.

Joining the Blocks Together

1. Build Rows 1 and 3 as follows: Block A, Block B, Block A, Block B.
2. Build Rows 2 and 4 as follows: Block B, Block A, Block B, Block A.
3. Join the rows together in order. The quilt top should measure 64½" square.

Border

From Fabric 1:

Cut 8 — 4½" strips

1. Join the strips together on the diagonal.
2. Cut 2 — 64½" lengths and attach to the top and bottom of the quilt top.

3. Cut 2 — 72½" lengths and attach to the sides of the quilt top. The quilt top should now measure 72½" square.

Appliqué

Follow **Hand Appliqué** instructions, page 5, to prepare and stitch down the appliqué shapes.

From Fabric 4:

Cut 5 large lily petals and 5 small lily petals

From Fabric 6:

Cut 5 large outer centers and 5 small centers

From Fabric 1:

Cut 5 large inner centers

Appliqué lily petals first, then large outer and small centers and then large inner centers.

Binding

From Fabric 1:

Cut 8 - 2½" strips

Follow **Quilting**, page 60, to mark, layer and quilt as desired. Follow **Making Binding**, page 62, to prepare, attach and complete binding.

Appliqué Placement Diagram

10

Fabric Requirements

 *Fabric 1 - 2⅜ yds for Blocks A & B, Border and Binding

 Fabric 2 - 1¾ yds for Blocks A & B

 Fabric 3 - ¼ yd for Block A

 Fabric 4 - 1 yd for Appliqué

* see below

 *Fabric 5 - yardage included above

 *Fabric 6 - ⅛ yd for Appliqué

 *Fabric 7 - ⅝ yd for Block A

 Fabric 8 - 1⅝ yds for Blocks A & B

 *Fabric 9 - ¼ yd for Block B & Appliqué

You will also need:
4½ yds Backing Fabric
80" square batting
Freezer Paper
Water Soluble Liquid Basting Glue

This alternate color combination uses the fabrics a little bit differently by repeating the border fabric in Blocks A and B. The border fabric is <u>not</u> used in the Buds Section of the Blocks or in the centers of the flowers. Instead an additional fabric has been added for the extra contrast. A "*" next to the description indicates that the fabric is used differently. Refer to the picture before cutting. Where there is no "*", the fabric usage is the same.

Family Room
Lily's Table Runner

Fabric Requirements

Finished Size: 20" x 52"
Finished Block Size: 16" square
Yardage is based on
43"/44" wide fabric

 Fabric 1 – ⅜ yd for Binding and Appliqué

 Fabric 2 – ⅜ yd for Blocks A & B

 Fabric 3 – ⅛ yd for Block B

 Fabric 4 – ¼ yd for Appliqué

 Fabric 5 – ½ yd for Blocks A & B

 Fabric 6 – ⅛ yd for Appliqué

 Fabric 7 – 2/3 yd for Blocks A & B and Border

You will also need:
1⅝ yds Backing Fabric
28" x 60" batting
Freezer Paper
Liquid Water Soluble Basting Glue

Cutting for Blocks

Follow **Rotary Cutting**, page 58, to cut pieces. Cut all strips from the selvage-to-selvage width of fabric. All measurements include ¼" seam allowances.

From Fabric 2:
Cut 4 - 1½" strips
    Sub-cut 24 - 1½" x 2½" rectangles
    24 - 1½" x 3½" rectangles
    2 - 1½" x 10½" rectangles
Cut 1 - 2½" strip
    Sub-cut 4 - 2½" squares
    2 - 1½" x 2½" rectangles
Cut 1 - 2⅞" strip
    Sub-cut 4 - 2⅞" squares

From Fabric 3:
Cut 1 - 2½" strip
    Sub-cut 4 - 2½" squares

From Fabric 5:
Cut 1 - 8½" strip
    Sub-cut 2 - 8½" x 12½" rectangles
    1 - 8½" x 16½" rectangle
Cut 2 - 2½" strips
    Sub-cut 10 - 2½" squares
    2 - 2½" x 10½" rectangles

From Fabric 7:
Cut 2 - 1½" strips
    Sub-cut 10 - 1½" x 4½" rectangles
    2 - 1½" x 12½" rectangles
Cut 2 - 2½" x strips
    Sub-cut 16 - 2½" x 3½" rectangles
Cut 1 - 2⅞" strip
    Sub-cut 4 - 2⅞" squares

Building Block A (2)

Follow **Machine Piecing** and **Pressing**, pages 58 & 60, to assemble quilt top. Measure your work as you go to ensure that it matches the measurements provided and adjust your seam allowances as needed.

1. Attach a 1½" x 2½" Fabric 2 rectangle to one end of 12 - 2½" x 3½" Fabric 7 rectangles. Set aside.
2. Attach a 1½" x 2½" Fabric 2 rectangle to the top of 10 - 2½" Fabric 5 squares.
3. Attach a 1½" x 3½" Fabric 2 rectangle to either side of the step 2 units.
4. Attach a 1½" x 4½" Fabric 7 rectangle to the top of the step 3 units.
5. Join the step 1 units and the step 4 units into 2 - 5A units, 2 - 5B units and 2 - 5C units as shown. Set aside.

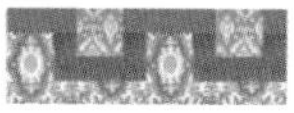

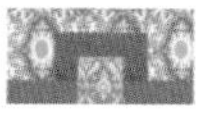

| 5A | 5B | 5C |

6. Draw a diagonal line on the wrong side of 4 - 2⅞" Fabric 2 squares. Place the Fabric 2 squares on top of 4 - 2⅞" Fabric 7 squares. Using the diagonal line as a guide, sew a scant ¼" seam on either side of the line. Cut along the drawn line and press the squares open. You should have 8 squares measuring 2½" square. Trim if necessary.
7. Attach a 2½" Fabric 3 square to the top of 4 green and blue triangle squares and a 2½" Fabric 2 square to the bottom of the remaining 4 green and blue triangle squares as shown. Join the units together to form 4 Flower Bud Units. 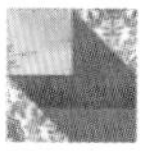
8. Using the picture of Block A as a guide, join a Flower Bud Unit to the left end of each of the 5A units and 5B units. Attach the 5C units to the left edge of each of the 8½" x 12½" Fabric 5 rectangles.
9. Attach the 3 rows together to form Block A.

Building Block B (1)

1. Attach a 1½" x 2½" Fabric 2 rectangle to one end of 4 - 2½" x 3½" Fabric 7 rectangles. Set aside.
2. Attach a 1½" x 10½" Fabric 2 rectangle to the top of 2 - 2½" x 10½" Fabric 5 rectangles and then a 1½" x 3½" Fabric 2 rectangle to either end of these units.
3. Attach a 1½" x 12½" Fabric 7 rectangle to the Fabric 2 edge of the Step 2 rectangles.
4. Using the picture of Block B as a guide, attach the step 1 rectangles to either end of the step 3 rectangle units. Attach these units to the top and bottom of the 8½" x 16½" Fabric 5 rectangle to complete Block B.
5. Attach a Block A to either end of the Block B. The center of the table runner should measure 16½" x 48½".

Border

From Fabric 7:

Cut 4 – 2½" strips

1. From 1 of the strips, cut 2 – 16½" lengths and attach to the ends of the table runner.
2. Join the remaining 3 strips together on the diagonal and cut 2 – 52½" lengths and attach to the top and bottom of the table runner. The table runner should now measure 20½" x 52½".

Appliqué

Follow **Hand Appliqué**, page 5, to prepare and stitch down the appliqué shapes.

From Fabric 4:

Cut 1 large lily petals and 2 small lily petals

From Fabric 6:

Cut 1 large outer centers and 2 small centers

From Fabric 1:

Cut 1 large inner centers

Appliqué lily petals first, then large outer and small centers and then large inner centers.

Binding

From Fabric 1:

Cut 4 – 2¼" strips

Follow **Quilting**, page 60, to mark, layer and quilt as desired. Follow **Making Binding**, page 62, to prepare, attach and complete binding.

Appliqué Placement Diagram

Guest Room
Danielle's Quilt

Fabric Requirements

Finished Quilt Size: 87" x 97"
Finished Block Size: 8"
Yardage is based on
43"/44" wide fabric

 Fabric 1 - 2½ yds for Block B and Outer Border

 Fabric 2 - 1 yd for Block B

 Fabric 3 - 2⅜ yds for Sashing and First Border

 Fabric 4 - ⅝ yd for Block A

 Fabric 5 - 4¼ yds for Block A, Block B, Sashing, Second Border and Binding

 Fabric 6 - ¾ yd for Block A

You will also need:
8 yds Backing Fabric
95" x 105 " batting

Cutting for Block A (28)

Follow **Rotary Cutting**, page 58, to cut pieces. Cut all strips from the selvage-to-selvage width of fabric. All measurements include ¼" seam allowances.

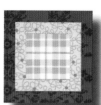

From Fabric 4:

Cut 4 - 4½" strips
 Sub-cut 28 - 4½" squares

From Fabric 6:

Cut 16 - 1½" strips
 Sub-cut 56 - 1½" x 4½" rectangles
  56 - 1½" x 6½" rectangles

From Fabric 5:

Cut 21 - 1½" strips
 Sub-cut 56 - 1½" x 6½" rectangles
  56 - 1½" x 8½" rectangles

Building Block A

Follow **Machine Piecing** and **Pressing**, pages 58 & 60, to assemble quilt top. Measure your work as you go to ensure that it matches the measurements provided and adjust your seam allowances as needed.

1. Attach the 1½" x 4½" Fabric 6 rectangles to the top and bottom of the 4½" Fabric 4 squares.
2. Attach the 1½" x 6½" Fabric 6 rectangles to the sides of the center blocks.
3. Attach the 1½" x 6½" Fabric 5 rectangles to the top and bottom of the center square units.
4. Attach the 1½" x 8½" rectangles to either side of the Block A units. Put aside.

Cutting for Block B (28)

From Fabric 1:

Cut 5 - 6½" strips
 Sub-cut 28 - 6½" squares

From Fabric 5:

Cut 19 - 1" strips
 Sub-cut 112 - 1" x 6½" rectangles

From Fabric 2:

Cut 21 - 1½" strips
 Sub-cut 56 - 1½" x 6½ rectangles
  56 - 1½" x 8½" rectangles

Building Block B

1. Press the 1" x 6½" rectangles in half lengthwise so that they measure ½" wide
2. Attach a 1" folded rectangle to the top and bottom of the 6½ Fabric 1 squares matching raw edges so that the Fabric 5 rectangle forms a flap. Repeat for the

sides of the squares. The center square should still measure 6½ square.

3. Attach the 1½" x 6½" Fabric 2 rectangles to the top and bottom of the center squares.
4. Attach the 1½" x 8½" Fabric 2 rectangles to the sides of the center squares.

Cutting for Sashing

From Fabric 3:

Cut 3 - 1½" strips
 Sub-cut 34 - 1½" x 2½" rectangles
  4 - 1½" squares
Cut 26 - 2½" strips
 Sub-cut 127 - 2½" x 8½" rectangles

From Fabric 5:

Cut 27 - 1½" strips
 Sub-cut 576 - 1½" squares
  30 - 1½" x 8½" rectangles
Cut 5 - 2½" strips
 Sub-cut 72 - 2½" squares

Fig. 1

Building the Sashing

1. There are 127 sashing rectangle units (Fig. 1).
2. Draw a diagonal line on the wrong side of each of the 1½" Fabric 5 squares. Put aside 68 of the squares to be used later on.
3. Place a 1½" Fabric 5 square on the upper left hand corners and lower right hand corners of the 2½" x 8½" Fabric 3 rectangles as shown so that the diagonal lines are oriented as in Fig. 2.

Fig. 2

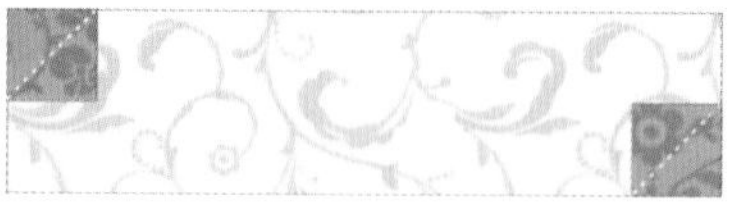

4. Sew along the diagonal lines. Trim the corners to within ¼" from the sewing line and press the Fabric 5 squares into the corners to complete the shape of the rectangle.
5. Place another two 1½" squares this time in the upper right and lower left hand corners (Fig. 3).

Fig. 3

6. Sew along the diagonal lines, trim and press. The finished sashing units should measure 2½" x 8½".

Building Block Rows 1, 3, 5 and 7

1. Begin building Block Row 1 by attaching a 2½" x 8½" sashing unit to the right side of a 1½" x 8½" Fabric 5 rectangle.
2. Next join a Block A to the right side of the sashing unit.
3. Continue on down the row adding sashing units in between alternating Block A's and B's.
4. End the row by adding a 1½" x 8½" Fabric 5 rectangle on the right side of the final sashing unit.
5. The completed row should measure 8½" x 74½".
6. Repeat instructions in paragraphs 1 to 5 to construct rows 3, 5 and 7.

Building Block Rows 2, 4, 6 and 8

1. Build Block Row 2 in the same manner as Row 1. This time, however, add Block B to the right side of the first sashing unit as shown in the Queen Size Layout.
2. The completed Row 2 should measure 8½" x 74½".
3. Repeat row construction to complete Rows 4, 6 and 8. Set aside.

Building the Sashing Rows

1. There are 9 Sashing Rows in the quilt top. The Sashing Rows separate the Block Rows and sit above Block Row 1 and below Block Row 8. They are made up of 2 end units, 7 sashing units and 8 squares.
2. Begin by building 34 end units. When the end units are complete, put 16 aside to building the Sashing End Rows.
3. Place 34 - 1½" Fabric 5 squares on the top half of a 34 - 1½" x 2½" Fabric 3 rectangles (Fig.4).
4. Sew along the dotted line. Trim the corner to within ¼" of the sewing line and press the Fabric 5 square into the corner.
5. Place the remaining 1½" Fabric 5 squares on the bottom half of the end units. Again sew along the dotted line, trim and press.

Fig. 4

6. Build the Sashing Rows by attaching a 2½" Fabric 5 square to the right of an end unit so that the points of the end unit are pointing away from the square (Fig.5).

Fig. 5

7. Attach a sashing unit to the right of the 2½" Fabric 5 square, then another square, then another sashing etc. until all 7 sashing units are joined with all 8 squares. End the rows with an end unit. Attach the end unit so that the points are pointing away from the final squares. The completed Sashing Rows should measure 2½" x 74½".

Building the Sashing End Rows

1. The Sashing End Rows sit above the first Sashing Row and below the last Sashing Row in order to complete the star pattern.
2. Attach an end unit to the right side of a 1½" Fabric 3 square so the points of the end unit are pointing up.

3. Then attach a 1½" x 8½" Fabric 5 rectangle to the right side of the end unit. Always adding to the right, alternate end units with 1½" x 8½" Fabric 5 rectangles until you have joined a total of 8 end units and 7 rectangles ending with an end unit.
4. Add a 1½" Fabric 3 square to the end of the row to complete the Sashing End Row which should measure 1½" x 74½" long.
5. Repeat instructions to build the other Sashing End Row.

Putting the Rows and Sashing Together

1. Begin at the top of the quilt. Attach a Sashing Row to the bottom of a Sashing End Row.
2. Add Block Row 1 to the bottom of the Sashing Row.
3. Add another Sashing Row to the bottom of Block Row 1 and then add Block Row 2 etc. continuing on until Block Row 8 and the final Sashing Row has been attached. Complete the center of the quilt top by adding the 2nd Sashing End Row.
4. The quilt top should now measure 74½" x 84½".

First Border
From Fabric 3:
Cut 8 – 1½" strips
1. Join the strips together on the diagonal.
2. Cut 2 – 1½" x 74½" lengths and attach to the top and bottom of the quilt top.
3. Cut 2 – 1½" x 86½" lengths and attach to the sides of the quilt top.
4. The quilt top should now measure 76½" x 86½".

Second Border
From Fabric 5:
Cut 9 – 2" strips
1. Join the strips together on the diagonal. Fold and press the strips in half lengthwise so the strip measures 1" wide. (This is done to prevent this long narrow border from stretching)
2. Cut 2 – 1" x 76½" lengths and attach to the top and bottom of the quilt top.
3. Cut 2 – 1" x 87½" lengths and attach to the sides of the quilt top.
4. The quilt top should now measure 77½ x 87½".

Third Border
From Fabric 1:
Cut 10 – 5½" strips
1. Join the strips together on the diagonal.
2. Cut 2 – 5½" x 77½" lengths and attach to the top and bottom of the quilt top.
3. Cut 2 – 5½" x 97½" lengths and attach to the sides of the quilt top.
4. The quilt top should now measure 87½" x 97½".

Binding
From Fabric 5:
Cut 10 – 2½" strips
Follow **Quilting**, page 60, to mark, layer and quilt as desired. Follow **Making Binding**, page 62, to prepare, attach and complete binding.

22

Guest Room
Danielle's Quilt
Lap Size

Fabric Requirements

Finished Quilt Size: 67" x 77"
Finished Block Size: 8"
Yardage is based on
43"/44" wide fabric

 Fabric 1 - 1⅞ yds for Block B and Outer Border

 Fabric 2 - ½ yd for Block B

 Fabric 3 - 1½ yds for Sashing and First Border

 Fabric 4 - ⅜ yd for Block A

 Fabric 5 - 2¾ yds for Block A, Block B, Sashing, Second Border and Binding

 Fabric 6 - ½ yd for Block A

You will also need:
4¼ yd Backing Fabric
75" x 85" batting

Read the following in connection with the instructions for the queen size version of this quilt beginning on page 16.

Cutting For Block A (15)

From Fabric 4:
Cut 2 – 4½" strips
    Sub-cut 15 – 4½" squares
From Fabric 5:
Cut 11 – 1½" strips
    Sub-cut 30 – 1½" x 6½" rectangles
    30 – 1½" x 8½" rectangles
From Fabric 6:
Cut 9 – 1½" strips
    Sub-cut 30 – 1½" x 4½" rectangles
    30 – 1½" x 6½" rectangles

Cutting For Block B (15)

From Fabric 1:
Cut 3 – 6½" strips
    Sub-cut 15 – 6½" squares
From Fabric 2:
Cut 11 – 1½" strips
    Sub-cut 30 – 1½" x 6½" rectangles
    30 – 1½" x 8½" rectangles
From Fabric 5:
Cut 10 – 1" strips
    Sub-cut 60 – 1" x 6½" rectangles

Cutting For Sashing

There are 71 sashing units and 7 sashing rows.
From Fabric 3:
Cut 2 – 1½" strips
    Sub-cut 26 – 1½" x 2½" rectangles
    4 – 1½" squares
Cut 15 – 2½" strips
    Sub-cut 71 – 2½" x 8½" rectangles

From Fabric 5:
Cut 17 – 1½" strips
    Sub-cut 336 – 1½" squares
    22 – 1½" x 8½" rectangles
Cut 3 – 2½" strips
    Sub-cut 42 – 2½" squares

Cutting For First Border

From Fabric 3:
Cut 6 – 1½" strips
    Sub-cut 2 – 54½" lengths, and
      2 – 66½" lengths

Cutting For Second Border

From Fabric 5:
Cut 6 – 2" strips
    Sub-cut 2 – 1" x 56½" lengths*
      2 – 1" x 67½" lengths*
*strips are folded in half lengthwise to prevent stretching

Cutting For Third Border

From Fabric 1:
Cut 8 – 5½" strips
    Sub-cut 2 – 57½" lengths
    2 – 77½" lengths

Cutting For Binding

From Fabric 5:
Cut 8 – 2½" strips

Guest Room
Danielle's Pillow

Fabric Requirements

Finished Pillow Size: 21" x 41"
Finished Block Size: 8"
Yardage is based on
43"/44" wide fabric

 Fabric 1 - ⅜ yd for Block B, Sashing and Third Border

 Fabric 2 - ⅛ yd for Block B

 Fabric 3 - ¼ yd for Sashing and First Border

 Fabric 4 - Fat ⅛th for Block A

 Fabric 5 - ⅝ yd for Blocks A & B, Sashing and Second Border

 Fabric 6 - ⅛ yd for Block A

 Fabric 7 - 1½ yds for Outer Border and Backing

You will also need:
29" x 49" piece of muslin
29" x 49" piece of batting
21" x 41" pillow insert*

*see instructions in pull out section

Cutting for Block A (2)

Follow **Rotary Cutting**, page 58, to cut pieces. Cut all strips from the selvage-to-selvage width of fabric. All measurements include ¼" seam allowances.

From Fabric 4:

Cut 1 – 4½" strip
Sub-cut 2 – 4½" squares

From Fabric 5:

Cut 2 – 1½" strip
Sub-cut 4 – 1½" x 6½" rectangles
4 – 1½" x 8½" rectangles

From Fabric 6:

Cut 2 – 1½" strip
Sub-cut 4 – 1½" x 4½" rectangles
4 – 1½" x 6½" rectangles

Building Block A

Follow **Machine Piecing** and **Pressing**, pages 58 & 60, to assemble quilt top. Measure your work as you go to ensure that it matches the measurements provided and adjust your seam allowances as needed.

Build the two Block A's, following the instructions on page 18.

Cutting for Block B (1)

From Fabric 1:

Cut 1 – 6½" strip
Sub-cut 1 – 6½" square
4 – 2½" squares
(set aside for Third Border)

1 – 2½" x 21½" rectangle
(set aside for backing trim)

From Fabric 2:

Cut 1 – 1½" strip
Sub-cut 2 – 1½" x 6½" rectangles
2 – 1½" x 8½" rectangles

From Fabric 5:

Cut 1 – 1" strip
Sub-cut 4 – 1" x 6½" rectangles

Building Block B

Build one Block B, following the instructions on page 18.

Cutting for Sashing

From Fabric 1:

Cut 2 – 2½" strips
Sub-cut 10 – 2½" x 8½" rectangles

From Fabric 3:

Cut 1 – 1½" strip
Sub-cut 4 – 1½" squares
12 – 1½" x 2½" rectangles

From Fabric 5:

Cut 4 – 1½" strips
Sub-cut 64 – 1½" squares
8 – 1½" x 8½" rectangles

Cut 1 – 2½" strip
Sub-cut 8 – 2½" squares

Building the Center of the Pillow

1. Build 10 Sashing Units following the instructions on page 18.
2. The pillow features one Block Row which is set between two Sashing Rows which are in turn set between two Sashing End Rows.
3. Build the Block Row by attaching a Sashing unit to right edge of a 1½" x 8½" Fabric 5 rectangle, then Block A, a Sashing Unit, Block B, a Sashing Unit, Block A, a Sashing Unit and then ending the Block Row with a 1½" x 8½" Fabric 5 rectangle.
4. Build 12 End Units by following the instructions beginning in paragraph 2 on page 19.
5. Build 2 Sashing Rows following the instructions beginning in paragraph 6 on page 19 but only joining 4 – 2½" Fabric 5 squares and 3 Sashing Units. The completed Sashing Rows should measure 2½" x 34½". Attach Sashing Rows to top and bottom of Block Row.
6. Build the two Sashing End Rows by following the instructions beginning on page 19 this time joining 4 end units and 3 – 1½" x 8½" Fabric 5 rectangles. Attach completed Sashing End Rows to top and bottom of pillow center.

Cutting for First Border
From Fabric 3:
Cut 3 – 1½" strips
1. Cut 2 – 34½" lengths and attach to the top and bottom of the pillow front.
2. Cut 2 – 16½" lengths and attach to the sides of the pillow front.
3. Pillow front should now measure 16½" x 36½".

Cutting for Second Border
From Fabric 5:
Cut 3 – 2" strips
1. Press the strips in half lengthwise. This will help prevent the narrow border from stretching.
2. Cut 2 – 1" x 36½" lengths and attach to the top and bottom of the pillow front.
3. Cut 2 – 1" x 17½" lengths and attach to sides of the pillow front.
4. The pillow front should now measure 17½" x 37½".

Cutting for Third Border
Cutting from Fabric 7:
Cut 3 – 2½" strips
1. Cut 2 – 37½" lengths and attach to the top and bottom of the pillow front.
2. Cut 2 – 17½" lengths. Attach a 2½" Fabric 1 square to either end of both lengths. Attach to sides of pillow front.
3. The pillow front should now measure 21½" x 41½".

Quilting the Pillow Front
Use the muslin as a backing and follow **Quilting**, page 60, to mark, layer and quilt as desired.

Backing
Follow **Pillows Without Binding**, page 61, to complete the backing and finish the pillow.
From Fabric 7:
Cut 2 – 21½" strips
    Sub-cut 1 – 21½" square (right panel)
    1 – 21½" x 31½" rectangle (left panel)

Pillow Layout

Young Girl's Room
Holly's Quilt

Fabric Requirements

Finished Quilt Size: 79" x 99"
Finished Block Size: 9" square
Yardage is based on
43"/44" wide fabric

 Fabric 1 – 1¾ yds for Blocks A, F, G, H and I

 Fabric 2 – 1⅞ yd for Blocks, B, C, D, E, F, H and I

 Fabric 3 – ⅞ yd for Blocks A, D and G

 Fabric 4 – ¾ yd for Blocks C, D and E

 Fabric 5 – 2¼ yds for Blocks F & I, Sashing and Inner Border

 Fabric 6 – 2⅜ yds for Block G, Outer Border and Binding

 Fabric 7 – ⅜ yd for Block H

 Fabric 8 – 1⅛ yd for Blocks, A, B, C and E

 Fabric 9 – ¼ yd for Block I

You will also need:
7¼ yds Backing
87" x 107" batting
Freezer Paper
Water Soluble Liquid Basting Glue
Light Cardboard for Template

29

Cutting for Block A (4)

Follow **Rotary Cutting**, page 58, to cut pieces. Cut all strips from the selvage-to-selvage width of fabric. All measurements include ¼" seam allowances.

From Fabric 1:

Cut 1 - 10" strip
     Sub-cut 4 - 10" squares

From Fabric 8:

Cut 28 petals - Follow **Machine Appliqué**, page 4, to prepare and stitch down the appliqué shapes.

From Fabric 3:

Cut 4 flower centers - Follow **Gathered Circles Appliqué**, page 5, to prepare and stitch down the appliqué shapes.

Cutting for Block B (8)

From Fabric 2:

Cut 2 - 10" strips
     Sub-cut 8 - 10" squares

From Fabric 8:

Cut 56 petals

From Fabric 2:

Cut 8 flower centers

Cutting for Block C (4)

From Fabric 2:

Cut 1 - 10" strip
     Sub-cut 4 - 10" squares

From Fabric 4:

Cut 28 petals

From Fabric 8:

Cut 4 flower centers

Cutting for Block D (6)

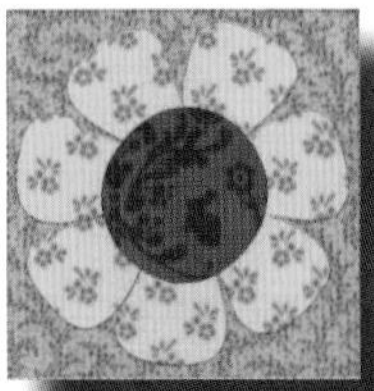

From Fabric 3:

Cut 2 - 10" strips
     Sub-cut 6 - 10" squares

From Fabric 4:

Cut 42 petals

From Fabric 2:

Cut 6 flower centers

Cutting for Block E (4)

From Fabric 2:

Cut 1 - 10" strip
     Sub-cut 4 - 10" squares

From Fabric 8:

Cut 28 petals

From Fabric 4:

Cut 4 flower centers

Building Blocks A – E

After you have attached the flowers to the backgrounds with your machine, trim the blocks so they measure 9½" square making sure the flowers remain centered in the blocks. Set aside.

Cutting for Block F (9)

Follow **Machine Piecing** and **Pressing**, pages 58 & 60, to assemble quilt top. Measure your work as you go to ensure that it matches the measurements provided and adjust your seam allowances as needed.

From Fabric 5:

Cut 2 - 3⅞" strips
     Sub-cut 18 - 3⅞" squares
Cut 2 - 4¼" strips
     Sub-cut 18 - 4¼" squares
Cut 1 - 3½" strip
     Sub-cut 9 - 3½" squares

From Fabric 1:

Cut 2 - 3⅞" strips
     Sub-cut 18 - 3⅞" squares
Cut 1 - 4¼" strip
     Sub-cut 9 - 4¼" squares

From Fabric 2:

Cut 1 - 4¼" strip
     Sub-cut 9 - 4¼" squares

Building Block F

1. Draw a diagonal line on the wrong side of each of the 4¼" Fabric 5 squares.
2. Place a 4¼" Fabric 5 square on top of each of the 9 - 4¼" Fabric 1 squares and each of the 9 - 4¼" Fabric 2 squares. Using the diagonal line as a guide, sew a scant ¼" seam on either side of the line. Cut along the drawn line and press the squares open. Trim the squares so they measure 3⅞" square. When complete, you should have 18 - 3⅞" green and brown triangle squares and 18 - 3⅞" green and yellow triangle squares.   Fig. 1
3. Draw a diagonal line on the wrong side of the green and yellow triangle squares so that the diagonal line crosses the seam line (Fig. 1). 
4. Place the yellow and green triangle squares on top of the green and brown triangle squares so that the green triangle in the top square is on the brown triangle in the bottom square and the yellow triangle

in the top square is on top of the green triangle in the bottom square. The diagonal seam lines of the top and bottom squares should be butted up against each other.

5. Using the drawn line as a guide, sew a scant ¼" seam on either side of the line. Cut along the drawn line and press the squares open. Trim the squares so they measure 3½" square. When complete, you should have 36 – 3½" quarter triangle squares.

6. Draw a diagonal line on the wrong side of each of the 3⅞" Fabric 5 squares.

7. Place the 3⅞" Fabric 5 squares on top of each of the 3⅞" Fabric 1 squares. Using the diagonal line as a guide, sew a scant ¼" seam on either side of the line. Cut along the drawn line and press the squares open. Trim the squares so they measure 3½" square. When complete, you should have 36 – 3½" green and yellow triangle squares.

8. Use the picture of Block F as a guide to assemble the block together, first in rows and then join the rows together.

Cutting for Block G (8)

Cut from Fabric 1:
Cut 2 – 3⅞" strips
    Sub-cut 16 – 3⅞" squares
From Fabric 3:
Cut 1 – 3½" strip
    Sub-cut into 8 – 3½" squares
From Fabric 6:
Cut 2 – 3⅞" strips
    Sub-cut 16 – 3⅞" squares
Cut 3 – 3½" strips
    Sub-cut 32 – 3½" squares

Building Block G

1. Draw a diagonal line on the wrong side of each of the 3⅞" Fabric 1 squares.

2. Place the 3⅞" Fabric 1 squares on top of each of the 3⅞" Fabric 6 squares. Using the diagonal line as a guide, sew a scant ¼" seam on either side of the line. Cut along the drawn line and press the squares open. Trim the squares so they measure 3½" square. When complete, you should have 32 – 3½" floral and dot triangle squares.

3. Use the picture of Block G as a guide to assemble the block together, first in rows and then join the rows together.

Cutting for Block H (12)

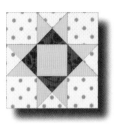

From Fabric 1:
Cut 4 – 3½" strips
    Sub-cut 48 – 3½" squares
Cut 2 – 4¼" strips
    Sub-cut 12 – 4¼" squares
From Fabric 2:
Cut 2 – 4¼" strips
    Sub-cut 12 – 4¼" squares
From Fabric 7:
Cut 2 – 4¼" strips
    Sub-cut 24 – 4¼" squares
Cut 1 – 3½" strips
    Sub-cut 12 – 3½" squares

Building Block H

1. Draw a diagonal line on the wrong side of each of the 4¼" Fabric 7 squares.

2. Place a 4¼" Fabric 7 square on top of each of the 9 – 4¼" Fabric 1 squares and each of the 9 – 4¼" Fabric 2 squares. Using the diagonal line as a guide, sew a scant ¼" seam on either side of the line. Cut along the drawn line and press the squares open. Trim the squares so they measure 3⅞" square. When complete, you should have 18 – 3⅞" pink and brown triangle squares and 18 – 3⅞" pink and yellow triangle squares.

3. Draw a diagonal line on the wrong side of the pink and yellow triangle squares so that the diagonal line crosses the seam line (see Fig. 1 under Block F).

4. Place the yellow and pink triangle squares on top of the pink and brown triangle squares so that the pink triangle in the top square is on the brown triangle in the bottom square and the yellow triangle in the top square is on top of the pink triangle in the bottom square. The diagonal seam lines of the top and bottom squares should be butted up against each other.

5. Using the drawn line as a guide, sew a scant ¼" seam on either side of the line. Cut along the drawn line and press the squares open. Trim the squares so they measure 3½" square. When complete, you should have 48 - 3½" quarter triangle squares.
6. Use the picture of Block H as a guide to assemble the block together, first in rows and then join the rows together.

Cutting for Block I (8)

From Fabric 1:
Cut 2 - 3⅞" strips
    Sub-cut 16 - 3⅞" squares
From Fabric 2:
Cut 3 - 3½" strips
    Sub-cut 32 - 3½" squares
From Fabric 5:
Cut 1 - 3½" strip
    Sub-cut 8 - 3½" squares
From Fabric 9:
Cut 2 - 3⅞" strips
    Sub-cut 16 - 3⅞" squares

Building Block I

1. Draw a diagonal line on the wrong side of each of the 3⅞" Fabric 1 squares.
2. Place the 3⅞" Fabric 1 squares on top of each of the 3⅞" Fabric 9 squares. Using the diagonal line as a guide, sew a scant ¼" seam on either side of the line. Cut along the drawn line and press the squares open. Trim the squares so they measure 3½" square. When complete, you should have 32 - 3½" yellow dot and yellow triangle squares.
3. Use the picture of Block I as a guide to assemble the block together, first in rows and then join the rows together.

Building the Rows

From Fabric 5:
Cut 14 - 1½" strips
    Sub-cut 54 - 9½" lengths
1. Using the Queen Size Layout as a guide, lay out Row 1 on the floor or on a design wall.

2. Place a 1½" x 9½" sashing strip between each of the blocks but not at the beginning or the end of the row.
3. Join the blocks and sashing strips together. Label the row as Row 1. The row should measure 9½" x 69½".
4. Repeat for the remaining 8 rows labelling them as you go.

Putting the Rows Together

From Fabric 5:
Cut 22 - 1½" strips
1. Join all of the strips together on the diagonal. Cut 10 - 69½" lengths and 2 - 91½" lengths.
2. Attach a 69½" length to the top and bottom of Row 1, pinning the sashing in place.
3. Pin Row 2 to the bottom of the sashing below Row 1. Line up the vertical sashing bars in the two rows as you pin to ensure that the blocks are lined up properly. Sew in place.
4. Continue adding sashing and block rows until you have added the last sashing row at the bottom of the quilt.
5. Attach the 1½" x 91½" sashing lengths to the sides of the quilt top which should now measure 71½" x 91½".

Outer Border

From Fabric 6:
Cut 9 - 4½" strips
1. Join the strips together on the diagonal. Cut 2 - 4½" x 71½" lengths and attach to the top and bottom of the quilt top. Cut 2 - 4½" x 99½" lengths and attach to the sides of the quilt top.
2. The quilt top should now measure 79½" x 99½".

Binding

From Fabric 6:
Cut 9 - 2½" strips
Follow **Quilting**, page 60, to mark, layer and quilt as desired. Follow **Making Binding**, page 62, to prepare, attach and complete binding.

Holly's Quilt
Lap Size

Fabric Requirements

Finished Quilt Size: 59" x 79"
Finished Block Size: 9"
Yardage is based on
43"/44" wide fabric

 Fabric 1 – ⅞ yd for Blocks F, G, H and I

 Fabric 2 – 1¼ yds for Blocks A, B and G

 Fabric 3 – 1½ yds for Blocks A and H and Binding

 Fabric 4 – ⅜ yd for Block B

 Fabric 5 – ½ yd for Blocks F, H and I

 Fabric 6 – ¼ yd for Blocks A and B

 Fabric 7 – ¼ yd for Block I

 Fabric 8 – 1⅜ yds for Block F and I, Sashing and Inner Border

 Fabric 9 – ½ yd for Block G

 Fabric 10 – 1 yd for Outer Border

You will also need:
3⅞ yd Backing Fabric
67" x 87" batting
Freezer Paper
Water Soluble Liquid Basting Glue
Light Cardboard for Template

When building Blocks, refer to pictures of Blocks on page 36 as some of the fabrics used in the sample are not exactly as shown here. Read the following in connection with the instructions for the double size version of this quilt beginning on page 28.

Cutting for Block A (8)
From Fabric 3:
Cut 2 - 10" strips
    Sub-cut 8 - 10" squares
From Fabric 2:
Cut 56 petals
From Fabric 6:
Cut 8 flower centers

Cutting for Block B (6)
From Fabric 2:
Cut 2 - 10" strip
    Sub-cut 6 - 10" squares
From Fabric 4:
Cut 42 petals
From Fabric 6:
Cut 6 flower centers

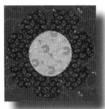

There are no Block C's, D's or E's in the lap size

Cutting for Block F (1)
From Fabric 8:
Cut 1 - 3⅞" strips
    Sub-cut 2 - 3⅞" squares
Cut 1 - 4¼" strips
    Sub-cut 2 - 4¼" squares
Cut 1 - 3½" strip
    Sub-cut 9 - 3½" squares
    (set aside 8 squares for Block I)
From Fabric 1:
Cut 3 - 3⅞" strips
    Sub-cut 26 - 3⅞" squares
    (set aside 8 squares for Block G, and
     16 squares for Block I)
Cut 1 - 4¼" strip
    Sub-cut 9 - 4¼" squares
    (set aside 8 squares for Block H)
From Fabric 5:
Cut 1 - 4¼" strip
    Sub-cut 9 - 4¼" squares
    (set aside 8 squares for Block H)

Cutting for Block G (4)
From Fabric 1:
Use 8 - 3⅞" squares from
cutting for Block F
From Fabric 2:
Cut 1 - 3½" strip
    Sub-cut 4 - 3½" squares
From Fabric 9:
Cut 2 - 3⅞" strips

Sub-cut 8 - 3⅞" squares
Cut 2 - 3½" strips
    Sub-cut 16 - 3½" squares

Cutting for Block H (8)
From Fabric 1:
Cut 3 - 3½" strips
    Sub-cut 32 - 3½" squares
Use 8 - 4¼" squares from
cutting for Block F
From Fabric 5:
Use 8 - 4¼" squares from cutting for Block F
From Fabric 3:
Cut 2 - 4¼" strips
    Sub-cut 16 - 4¼" squares
Cut 1 - 3½" strips
    Sub-cut 8 - 3½" squares

Cutting for Block I (8)
From Fabric 1:
Use 16 - 3⅞" squares from
cutting for Block F
From Fabric 8:
Use 8 - 3½" squares from
cutting for Block F
From Fabric 5:
Cut 3 - 3½" strips
    Sub-cut 32 - 3½" squares
From Fabric 7:
Cut 2 - 3⅞" strips
    Sub-cut 16 - 3⅞" squares

Cutting for Sashing and Inner Border
From Fabric 8:
Cut 21 - 1½" strips
    Sub-cut 28 - 1½" x 9½" rectangles
    8 - 49½" lengths, and
    2 - 71½" lengths for sashing rows
    and inner border

Cutting for Outer Border
From Fabric 10:
Cut 7 - 4½" strips
    Sub-cut 2 - 51½" lengths, and
      2 - 79½" lengths

Cutting for Binding
From Fabric 3:
Cut 7 - 2½" strips

Holly's Pillow

Fabric Requirements

Fabric 1 - ¼ yd for Binding

Fabric 2 - ½ yd for Backing and Backing

Fabric 3 - ⅜ yd for Petals and Backing Trim

Fabric 4 - Fat Eighth for Flower Center

You will also need
15" pillow form
14" square Fusible Polar Fleece
Freezer Paper
Light Cardboard for Template

Cutting for Pillow

Follow **Rotary Cutting**, page 58, to cut pieces. Cut all strips from the selvage-to-selvage width of fabric. All measurements include ¼" seam allowances.

From Fabric 1:
Cut 2 - 2¼" strips for binding

From Fabric 2:
Cut 1 - 16" strip
    Sub-cut 1 - 16" square, and
    1 - **15½" x 10"** rectangle (right back panel)
    1 - **15½" x 9"** rectangle (left back panel)

From Fabric 3:
Cut 16 petals (see paragraphs 1 and 2 under Flower Center)
Cut 1 - 2½" x 15½" rectangle

From Fabric 4:
Cut 1 flower center (see paragraphs 1 and 2 under Flower Petals)

37

38

Flower Center

Follow the instructions under **Gathered Circles Appliqué**, page 5, to prepare the center circle templates A and B.

1. Use template A to cut out the fabric circle from Fabric 4.
2. Use template B to cut out a circle from the fusible polar fleece.
3. Place the fusible polar fleece circle on your ironing board with the fusible side facing up. Place the wrong side of the fabric circle on top of the polar fleece circle so that the polar fleece circle is centered under the fabric circle and the right side of the fabric is facing up.
4. Following manufacturer's instructions, press the top of the fabric circle with an iron to adhere the polar fleece. DO NOT PUT IRON DIRECTLY ON THE FLEECE.
5. Follow the instructions under **Gathered Circles Appliqué,** page 5, to gather the fabric around the edge of the polar fleece. The polar fleece is stiff enough so you do not need to use the B Template.

Flower Petals

1. Trace the pillow petal template and the pillow fleece template onto regular paper and cut out along the drawn line. Use a glue stick to paste them to light cardboard then cut them out again.
2. Use the pillow petal template to trace 16 petals on the wrong side of Fabric 3 and cut them out along the drawn line.
3. Group the petals into matching pairs.
4. Use the polar fleece petal template to trace and cut out 8 polar fleece petals.
5. Place the polar fleece petals on the ironing board so the fusible side is facing up. Center one petal from each fabric pairs on top of the polar fleece petals so the right side of the fabric petal is facing up. Press to adhere the fleece to the fabric petal. DO NOT PUT IRON DIRECTLY ON THE FLEECE.

6. Place the matching fabric petals on top of the fused petals so the right sides of the fabric petals are together.
7. Sew the pairs together with a scant ¼" seam leaving the bottom of the petal shapes open. Turn the petals and press gently.

Putting It Together

1. Find the center of the 16" Fabric 2 background square by folding it in half and then half again. Place the cardboard B template in the middle of the background square so that it is centered and trace the shape using a temporary marking pen or pencil.
2. Lay the petals around the circle shape and pin in place. Lay the center over the petals to make sure that all the unfinished ends of the petals will be hidden under the flower center.
3. When placement is confirmed, sew around the drawn circle to secure the petals to the background.
4. Using your free motion quilting foot, sew the petals to the background (Fig. 1)
5. Center the flower center over the petals. Attach to background using a machine blanket stitch.
6. Trim the background square so that it measures 15½" square.

Fig. 1

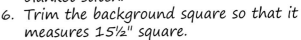

Backing and Binding

Follow **Pillows With Binding**, page 61, to complete the backing and finish the pillow.

40

Master Bedroom
Marcie's Quilt

Fabric Requirements

Finished Quilt Size: 82" x 90"
Finished Block Size: 8" square
Yardage is based on
43"/44" wide fabric

Fabric 1 – ⅝ yd for Block 1A

Fabric 2 – 1¼ yds for Outer Border

Fabric 3 – ⅝ yd for Block 1C

Fabric 4 – ⅝ yd for Block 1B

Fabric 5 – 1⅛ yds for Block 1C

Fabric 6 – 1⅛ yds for Block 1B

Fabric 7 – ¼ yd for Block 2A

Fabric 8 – 2⅞ yds for all Blocks

Fabric 9 – 1⅞ yds for all Block 2's, Inner Border and Binding

Fabric 10 – 1⅛ yds for Block 1A

Fabric 11 - ¼ yd for Block 2C

Fabric 12 - ¼ yd for Block 2A

Fabric 13 - ¼ yd for Block 2B

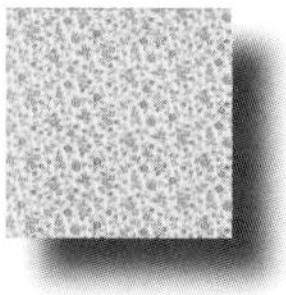

Fabric 14 - ¼ yd for Block 2C

Fabric 15 - ½ yd for all Block 2's

Fabric 16 - ¼ yd for Block 2B

You will also need:
90" x 98" batting
7½ yds Backing Fabric

Cutting for Block 1's

Follow **Rotary Cutting**, page 58, to cut pieces. Cut all strips from the selvage-to-selvage width of fabric. All measurements include ¼" seam allowances.

From Fabric 1:
Cut 3 - 6½" strips
    Sub-cut 14 - 6½" squares

From Fabric 3:
Cut 3 - 6½" strips
    Sub-cut 15 - 6½" squares

From Fabric 4:
Cut 3 - 6½" strips
    Sub-cut 16 - 6½" squares

From Fabric 8:
Cut 33 - 1½" strips
    Sub-cut 90 - 1½" x 6½" rectangles
    90 - 1½" x 8½" rectangles

From each of Fabric 5, 6 and 10:
Cut 1 - 37" square

Making Continuous Bias

Block 1's (Fig. 1 shows Block 1B) are framed squares with ruffle detailing around the center block which is made with continuous bias. Use the Fabric 5, 6 and 10 - 37" squares and following the instructions under **Making Continuous Bias** on page 59.

Fig. 1

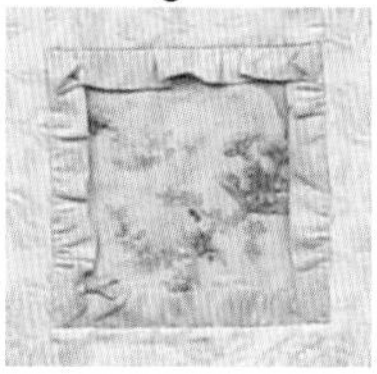

When complete, make the following cuts:

From Fabric 5 bias strip:
Cut 15 - 42" lengths

From Fabric 10 bias strip:
Cut 14 - 42" lengths

From Fabric 6 bias strip:
Cut 16 - 42" lengths

Building Blocks 1A (14), 1B (16) & 1C (15)

Follow **Machine Piecing** and **Pressing**, pages 58 & 60, to assemble quilt top. Measure your work as you go to ensure that it matches the measurements provided and adjust your seam allowances as needed.

1. Following the instructions under **"Making and Attaching Ruffles"**, page 59, to ruffle the bias strips down to 27". Attach the Fabric 10 ruffles to the 6½" Fabric 1 squares, the Fabric 5 ruffles to the 6½" Fabric 3 squares and the Fabric 6 ruffles to the 6½" Fabric 4 squares.

2. Complete the Block 1's by attaching a 1½" x 6½" Fabric 8 rectangle to the top and bottom of each of the ruffled squares and a 1½" x 8½" Fabric 8 rectangle to the sides of each of the ruffled squares.

Cutting for Block 2's

From Fabric 12:
Cut 2 - 2½" strips
    Sub-cut 30 - 2½" squares

From Fabric 7:
Cut 2 - 2½" strips
    Sub-cut 30 - 2½" squares

From Fabric 15:
Cut 6 - 2½" strips
    Sub-cut 90 - 2½" squares

From Fabric 9:
Cut 6 - 2½" strips
    Sub-cut 90 - 2½" squares

From Fabric 8:
Cut 20 - 2½" strips
    Sub-cut 180 - 2½" x 4½" rectangles

From Fabric 13:
Cut 2 - 2½" strips
    Sub-cut 28 - 2½" squares

From Fabric 16:
Cut 2 - 2½" strips
    Sub-cut 28 - 2½" squares

From Fabric 11:
Cut 2 - 2½" strips
    Sub-cut 32 - 2½" squares

From Fabric 14:
Cut 2 - 2½" strips
    Sub-cut 32 - 2½" squares

Building Blocks 2A (15), 2B (14) & 2C (16)

1. Following the Block 2A layout, piece the block together first by joining the four squares in the center together. Then attach Fabric 8 - 2½" x 4½" rectangles to the top and bottom of the four-square centers.

2A Layout

2B Layout

2. Add the appropriate squares on either end of two Fabric 8 rectangles and attach to the sides of the block. Repeat for remainder of the 2A Blocks.
3. Follow the 2B Layout and the 2C Layout to build the 2B and 2C Blocks.

2C Layout

Layout

1. Using the Queen Size Block Layout as a guide on page 44, join the blocks together in rows and then join the rows together.
2. When complete, the quilt top should measure 72½" x 80½".

Inner Border

From Fabric 9:
Cut 8 - 3" strips
1. Join the strips together on the diagonal and press in half lengthwise so the strip is now 1½" wide. (This will prevent the narrow border from stretching)
2. Sub-cut 2 - 72½" lengths. Attach to the top and bottom of the quilt top.
3. Sub-cut 2 - 82½" lengths. Attach to the sides of the quilt top.
4. The quilt top should now measure 74½" x 82½".

Outer Border

From Fabric 2:
Cut 9 - 4½" strips
1. Join the strips on the diagonal.
2. Sub-cut 2 - 74½" lengths and attach to the top and bottom of the quilt top.
3. Sub-cut 2 - 90½" lengths and attach to the sides of the quilt top.
4. The quilt top should now measure 82½" x 90½".

Quilting and Binding

From Fabric 9:
Cut 9 - 2½" strips
Follow **Quilting**, page 60, to mark, layer and quilt as desired. Follow **Making Binding**, page 62, to prepare, attach and complete binding.

Master Bedroom
Marcie's Pillows

Fabric Requirements

Pillow Sizes: 12" square & 12" x 24"
Yardage is based on
43"/44" wide fabric

12" Square Pillow

 Fabric 1 - Fat Eighth for center

 Fabric 2 - ⅛ yd for border

 Fabric 3 - ¾ yd for ruffle and backing

 Fabric 4 - ¼ yd for binding and trim on back

You will also need:
12" square pillow form

12" x 24" Pillow

 Fabric 1 - Fat Eighth for center

 Fabric 2 - ⅝ yd for border and backing

 Fabric 3 - ⅝ yd for ruffle, binding and trim on back

You will also need:
12" x 24" pillow form

Cutting for 12" Square Pillow
From Fabric 1:
Cut 1 - 6½" square
From Fabric 2:
Cut 1 - 3½" strip
    Sub-cut 2 - 3½" x 6½" rectangles
    2 - 3½" x 12½" rectangles

From Fabric 3:
Cut 1 - 10" square for continuous bias
Cut 1 - 12½" strip
    Sub-cut 1 - 8" x 12½" rectangle (right back panel)
    1 - 9" x 12½" rectangle (left back panel)
From Fabric 4:
Cut 2 - 2¼" strips
    Sub-cut 1 - 12½" strip for backing trim

Building the 12" Pillow

1. Make a continuous bias strip using the Fabric 3 - 10" squares and following the instructions under **Making Continuous Bias** on page 59. Cut a 42" length.
2. Following the instructions under **Making and Attaching Ruffles**, page 59, ruffle the bias strip down to 27" and then attach it to the 6½" Fabric 6 square.
3. Attach a 3½" x 6½" Fabric 2 rectangle to the sides of the center.
4. Attach a 3½" x 12½" rectangle to the top and bottom of the center.
5. The pillow front should measure 12½" square.

Backing

Follow **Pillows With Binding**, page 61, to complete the backing and finish the pillow.

Cutting for 12" x 24" Pillow

From Fabric 1:
Cut 1 - 6½" x 18½"
From Fabric 2:
Cut 2 - 3½" strip
    Sub-cut 2 - 3½" x 6½" rectangles
    2 - 3½" x 24½" rectangles

Cut 1 - 12½" strip
    Sub-cut 1 - 13" x 12½" rectangle (right back panel)
    1 - 17" x 12½" rectangle (left back panel)
From Fabric 3:
Cut 1 - 13" square for continuous bias
Cut 3 - 2¼" strips
    Sub-cut 1 - 12½" strip for backing trim

Building the 12" x 24" Pillow

1. Make a continuous bias strip using the Fabric 3 - 13" squares and following the instructions under **Making Continuous Bias** on page 59. Cut a 79" length.
2. Following the instructions under **Making and Attaching Ruffles**, page 59, ruffle the bias strip down to 51" and then attach it to the 6½" x 18½" rectangle.
3. Attach a 3½" x 6½" Fabric 2 rectangle to the sides of the center rectangle.
4. Attach a 3½" x 24½" rectangle to the top and bottom of the center rectangle.
5. The pillow should measure 12½" x 24½".

Backing

Follow **Pillows With Binding**, page 61, to complete the backing and finish the pillow.

Marcie's Quilt Baby Size

Fabric Requirements

Finished Quilt Size: 42" x 50"
Finished Block Size: 8"
Yardage is based on
43"/44" wide fabric

 Fabric 1 - ⅛ yd for Block 2A

 Fabric 2 - ⅛ yd for Block 2B

 Fabric 3 - ¼ yd for Blocks 2A & 2B

 Fabric 4 - ¾ yd for all Blocks

 Fabric 5 - ¼ yd for Block 1A

 Fabric 6 - ¼ yd for Block 1B

 Fabric 7 - 1 yd for Block 1C and Outer Border

 Fabric 8 - ½ yd for Block 1A

 Fabric 9 - ⅝ yd for Block 1B

 Fabric 10 - ½ yd for Block 1C

 Fabric 11 - ⅛ yd for Block 2A

 Fabric 12 - ⅛ yd for Block 2B

 Fabric 13 - ⅞ yd for Blocks 2A & 2B, Inner Border & Binding

You will also need:
2⅞ yds Backing Fabric
50" x 58" batting

Read the following in connection with the instructions for the queen size version of this quilt beginning on page 40.

Blocks 1A (3), 1B (4) and 1C (3)

Block 1A - Fabric 5 center with Fabric 8 ruffle
Block 1B - Fabric 6 center with Fabric 9 ruffle
Block 1C - Fabric 7 center with Fabric 10 ruffle.

Cutting for Block 1's

From Fabric 4:
Cut 8 - 1½" strips
    Sub-cut 20 - 1½" x 6½" rectangles
           20 - 1½" x 8½" rectangles
From each of Fabric 5 & 7:
Cut 1 - 6½" strip
    Sub-cut 3 - 6½" squares
From Fabric 6:
Cut 1 - 6½" strip
    Sub-cut 4 - 6½" squares
From each of Fabrics 8 & 10:
Cut 1 - 16" square for continuous bias
From Fabric 9"
Cut 1 - 19" square for continuous bias

Cutting for Block 2's

From each of Fabrics 1, 2, 11 & 12:
Cut 1 - 2½" strip
    Sub-cut each 10 - 2½" squares
From each of Fabrics 3 & 13:
Cut 2 - 2½" strips
    Sub-cut each 20 - 2½" squares
From Fabric 4:
Cut 5 - 2½" strips
    Sub-cut 40 - 2½" x 4½" rectangles

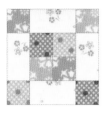

Block 2A

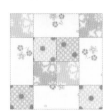

Block 2B

Cutting for Inner Border

From Fabric 13:
Cut 4 - 3" strips*
    Sub-cut 2 - 1½" x 32½" lengths
          2 - 1½" x 42½" lengths
(*press in half lengthwise)

Cutting for Outer Border

From Fabric 7:
Cut 5 - 4½" strips
    Sub-cut 2 - 34½" lengths
          2 - 50½" lengths

Cutting for Binding

From Fabric 13:
Cut 5 - 2½" strips

Block Layout

1B	2B	1C	2A
2A	1B	2B	1C
1A	2A	1B	2B
2B	1A	2A	1B
1C	2B	1A	2A

Young Boy's Room
Joey's Quilt

Fabric Requirements

Finished Quilt Size: 66" x 86"
Finished Block Size: 10" square
Yardage is based on
43"/44" wide fabric

 Fabric 1 – Fat Eighth for Dog Muzzle and Ears

 Fabric 2 – 1⅝ yds for Outer Border

 Fabric 3 – 2/3 yd for Dog and Bones

 Fabric 4 – 1 yd for Blocks F, G & H

 Fabric 5 – 1 yd for Blocks A, B, C, D & E

 Fabric 6 – 1⅛ yd for Inner Border and Binding

 Fabric 7 – 1/3 yd for Block G

Fabric 8 – ¼ yd for Block F

 Fabric 9 – ¼ yd for Block H

 Fabric 10 – ⅛ yd for Block E

 Fabric 11– ¼ yd for Block B

 Fabric 12 – ¼ yd for Block A

 Fabric 13 – ¼ yd for Block C

 Fabric 14 – ¼ yd for Block D

 Fabric 15 – Fat Quarter for Balls

 Fabric 16 – Fat Quarter for Balls and Tongue

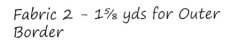

Fabric 17 - Fat Quarter for Balls

Fabric 18 - Fat Quarter for Balls, Nose, Spots & Eyes

You will also need:
5¼ yds backing fabric
74" x 94" batting
Freezer Paper for appliqué

Cutting for Center Blocks

Follow **Rotary Cutting**, page 58, to cut pieces. Cut all strips from the selvage-to-selvage width of fabric. All measurements include ¼" seam allowances.

From Fabric 5:
Cut 5 - 6½" strips
   Sub-cut 18 - 6½" x 10½" rectangles
From Fabric 4:
Cut 5 - 6½" strips
   Sub-cut 17 - 6½" x 10½" rectangles
From Fabric 12:
Cut 2 - 2½" strips
   Sub-cut 8 - 2½" x 10½" rectangles
From Fabric 11:
Cut 2 - 2½" strips
   Sub-cut 8 - 2½" x 10½" rectangles
From Fabric 13:
Cut 2 - 2½" strips
   Sub-cut 8 - 2½" x 10½" rectangles
From Fabric 14:
Cut 2 - 2½" strips
   Sub-cut 8 - 2½" x 10½" rectangles
From Fabric 10:
Cut 1 - 2½" strips
   Sub-cut 4 - 2½" x 10½" rectangles
From Fabric 8:
Cut 3 - 2½" strips
   Sub-cut 10 - 2½" x 10½" rectangles
From Fabric 7:
Cut 4 - 2½" strips
   Sub-cut 14 - 2½" x 10½" rectangles
From Fabric 9:
Cut 3 - 2½" strips
   Sub-cut 10 - 2½" x 10½" rectangles

Building the Center Blocks

Follow **Machine Piecing** and **Pressing**, pages 58 & 60, to assemble quilt top. Measure your work as you go to ensure that it matches the measurements provided and adjust your seam allowances as needed.

All of the blocks in the center will be labelled from A - H. To build the blocks, attach the appropriate 2½" x 10½" rectangles to either side of the appropriate 6½" x 10½" rectangle.

Block A (4)

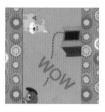

Block B (4)

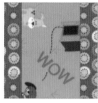

Block C (4)

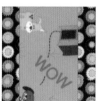

Block D (4)

Block E (2)

Block F (5)

Block G (7)

Block H (5)

Layout
1. Using the Block Layout Diagram below, join the blocks together in rows and then join the rows together.
2. When complete, the center of the quilt top should measure 50½" x 70½".

Inner Border
From Fabric 6:
Cut 7 – 2½" strips
1. Join the strips together on the diagonal.
2. Sub-cut 2 – 50½" lengths. Attach to the top and bottom of the quilt top.
3. Sub-cut 2 – 74½" lengths. Attach to the sides of the quilt top.
4. The quilt top should now measure 54½" x 74½".

Outer Border
From Fabric 2:
Cut 8 – 6½" strips
1. Join the strips together on the diagonal.
2. Sub-cut 2 – 54½" lengths. Attach to the top and bottom of the quilt top.
3. Sub-cut 2 – 86½" lengths. Attach to the sides of the quilt top.
4. The quilt top should now measure 66½" x 86½".

Appliqué
Follow **Rough Edge Appliqué**, page 4, to prepare and stitch down the appliqué shapes.
From Fabric 1:
Cut 1 muzzle, 1 inner right ear & 1 inner left ear
From Fabric 3:
Cut 1 dog body, 1 dog head, 1 right ear, 1 left ear, 1 tail, 2 small bones & 1 large bone
From Fabric 15:
Cut 3 Ball No.2's
From Fabric 16:
Cut 1 Ball No. 4, 1 Ball No.2 & 1 Tongue
From Fabric 17:
Cut 1 Ball No. 1 and 2 Ball No. 3's

From Fabric 18:
Cut 1 Ball No. 1, 1 Ball No. 2, 1 Ball No. 3, 1 Nose and 5 Spots & Eyes

Refer to the Appliqué Layout Diagram on page 54 to determine the placement of the appliqué shapes. The balls and bones can be attached in any order. Attach the dog appliqué shapes in the order set out below:
1. Tail
2. Right and Left Ear
3. Inner Right Ear and Inner Left Ear
4. Dog Body
5. Head
6. Tongue
7. Muzzle
8. Nose, Eyes and Spots

Binding
From Fabric 6:
Cut 8 – 2½" strips
Follow **Quilting**, page 60, to mark, layer and quilt as desired. Follow **Making Binding**, page 62, to prepare, attach and complete binding.

Block Layout Diagram

A	F	B	G	C
H	D	G	E	F
C	G	A	H	B
F	B	H	C	G
D	G	A	F	D
F	C	G	B	H
A	H	E	G	D

This version of Joey's Quilt is done in prints and plaids. The plaids are in the center of the squares replacing Fabrics 4 and 5. They are also used in the border and for some of the balls. The prints are used to frame the blocks, in the inner border and for the binding. A light print is used for the dog's eyes as contrast to the dark brown but black wool centers were added on top. A combination of red, green, blue, copper and beige make this quilt very cozy. A flannel backing would definitely make this quilt a favorite!

Young Boys's Room
Joey's Pillow

Fabric Requirements

Finished Pillow Size: 13" x 17"
Yardage is based on
43"/44" wide fabric

Fabric 1 - Fat Quarter for Background

Fabric 2 - ⅛ yd for Inner Border

Fabric 3 - ⅛ yd for Bone

Fabric 4 - ⅝ yd for Outer Border and Backing

Fabric 5 - ¼ yd for Binding

You will also need:
13" x 17" pillow form
21" x 25" piece of Muslin
21" x 25" piece of batting
Freezer Paper
Water Soluble Liquid Basting Glue

Cutting for Pillow

Follow **Rotary Cutting**, page 58, to cut pieces. Cut all strips from the selvage-to-selvage width of fabric. All measurements include ¼" seam allowances.

From Fabric 1:
Cut 1 - 8½" x 12½" rectangle

From Fabric 2:
Cut 2 - 1" strips
    Sub-cut 2 - 1" x 12½" rectangles
    2 - 1" x 9½" rectangles

From Fabric 3:
Cut 1 Small Bone - Follow **Rough Edge Appliqué**, page 4, to prepare the appliqué shape.

From Fabric 4:
Cut 2 - 2½" strips
    Sub-cut 4 - 2½" x 13½" rectangles
Cut 1 - 13½" strip
    Sub-cut 1 - 13½" square (left panel)
    1 - 13½" x 10" rectangle (right panel)

From Fabric 5:
Cut 2 - 2¼" strips for binding
    Sub-cut 1 - 2¼" x 13½" rectangle
    for backing trim

Building the Pillow

Follow **Machine Piecing** and **Pressing**, page 58 & 60, to assemble pillow top. Measure your work as you go to ensure that it matches the measurements provided and adjust your seam allowances as needed

1. Attach a 1" x 12½" Fabric 2 rectangle to the top and bottom of the 8½" x 12½" Fabric 1 background.
2. Attach a 1" x 9½" Fabric 2 rectangle to either side of the Fabric 1 background. Pillow should now measure 9½" x 13½".
3. Attach a 2½" x 13½" Fabric 4 rectangle to the top and bottom of the pillow center.
4. Attach the remaining 2½" x 13½" Fabric 4 rectangles to the sides of the pillow center. The pillow top should now measure 13½" x 17½".

Finishing the Pillow

Follow **Rough Edge Appliqué**, page 4, to stitch down the appliqué shapes. Follow **Quilting**, page 60, to mark, layer and quilt as desired. Follow **Pillows With Binding**, page 61, to complete the backing and finish the pillow.

General Instructions

To make your quilting easier and more enjoyable, we encourage you to carefully read all of the general instructions, study the color photographs, and familiarize yourself with the individual project instructions before beginning a project.

Fabrics

SELECTING FABRICS
- Choose high-quality, medium-weight 100% cotton fabrics.
- Yardage requirements listed for each project are based on 43"/44" wide fabric with a "usable" width of 42" after trimming selvages. Actual usable width will probably vary slightly from fabric to fabric. Our recommended yardage lengths should be adequate for occasional re-squaring of fabric when many cuts are required.

PREPARING FABRICS
We do not recommend washing fabrics before cutting as long as you are using high-quality "quilting" cotton. If you are not sure about the quality of your fabric or are concerned that the dye might run, pre-wash, dry and press.

Rotary Cutting
Rotary cutting has brought speed and accuracy to quilt making by allowing quilters to easily cut strips of fabric and then cut those strips into smaller pieces.
- Place fabric on work surface with fold closest to you.
- Cut all strips from the selvage-to-selvage width of the fabric unless otherwise indicated in project instructions.
- Square left edge of fabric using rotary cutter and rulers (**Figs. 1-2**)

Fig. 1

Fig. 2

- To cut each strip required for a project, place ruler over cut edge of fabric, aligning desired marking on ruler and cut edge; make cut (**Fig. 3**).

Fig. 3

- When cutting several strips from a single piece of fabric, it is important to make sure that cuts remain at a perfect right angle to the fold; square fabric as needed.

Machine Piecing
Precise cutting, followed by accurate piecing, will ensure that all pieces of your project fit together well.
- Set sewing machine stitch length for approximately 11 stitches per inch.
- Use neutral-colored cotton thread (not quilting thread) in needle and in bobbin.
- An accurate ¼" seam allowance is **essential**. Presser feet that are ¼" wide are available for most sewing machines. If not, mark

the ¼" seam with masking tape on the bed of your machine.

- When piecing, always place pieces right sides together (unless otherwise indicated in the pattern) and match raw edges; pin if necessary.
- Chain piecing saves time and will usually result in more accurate piecing.
- Trim away points of seam allowances that extend beyond edges of sewn pieces.
- A scant ¼" seam is slightly less than a full ¼" seam.
- The number in brackets (#) after cutting instructions or Block descriptions indicate the number of that block needed in the project.

SEWING ACROSS SEAM INTERSECTIONS

When sewing across the intersection of two seams, place pieces right sides together and match seams exactly, making sure seam allowances are pressed in opposite directions (**Fig. 4**).

Fig. 4

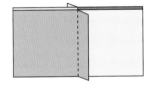

SEWING SHARP POINTS

To ensure sharp points when joining triangular or diagonal pieces, stitch across the center of the "X" (shown in pink) formed on wrong side by previous seams (**Fig. 5**).

Fig. 5

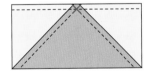

Making Continuous Bias

- Fold the fabric square along the diagonal and press fold. Open up the square and cut along the fold line. Place the top and bottom straight edges with right sides together, with triangle nubs overlapping equally at each end. Sew together with a ¼" seam allowance. Press open. On the

wrong side of the fabric, mark 2" lines parallel to the long angled edge (**Fig. 6**).

Fig. 6

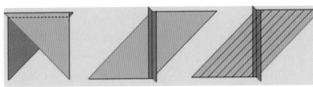

- Make a tube by bringing the right sides of the fabric together, offsetting the ends to make the lines match each other exactly. Sew the ends together with a ¼" seam allowance and press the seam open. Start cutting on one side of the tube, directly on a drawn line. Continue cutting around the tube until you have one long strip (**Fig. 7**).

Fig. 7

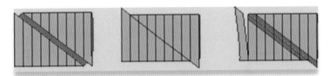

Making and Attaching Ruffles

- Cut length from continuous bias strip as indicated in the project.
- Fold strip in half lengthwise with wrong sides together and press.
- Using a long basting stitch, sew along the raw edge leaving a long tail of thread at either end of the strip.
- Pull the thread at one end of the strip to gather the raw edge of the bias strip to the length indicated in the project.
- Pin the ruffle strips to the outer edge of the background squares matching raw edges, overlapping the ends of the ruffle as shown (Fig. 8).

Fig. 8

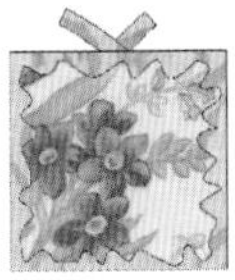

- Attach the ruffle to the background square or rectangle by sewing it down ⅛" in from the outer edge. (It is easier to keep the stitching line straight if you place the ruffle side down when sewing so the wrong side of the square is directly under the presser foot.) Pull out the basting thread and trim the overhanging ruffle. Lay the square down on an ironing board with the ruffle side down. Press the square using steam to flatten out the ruffle. The fold of the ruffle will be pressed toward the center of the block.

Pressing

- Use steam iron set on "Cotton" for all pressing.
- Press after sewing each seam.
- Seam allowances are almost always pressed to one side, usually toward darker fabric. However, to reduce bulk it may occasionally be necessary to press seam allowances toward the lighter fabric or even to press them open.
- To press long seams, such as those in long strip sets, without curving or other distortion, lay strips across width of the ironing board.

Machine Blanket Stitch

Some sewing machines feature a Blanket Stitch similar to the one used in this book. Refer to your owner's manual for machine set-up. If your machine does not have this stitch, try a zigzag stitch or any of the decorative stitches your machine has until you are satisfied with the look.

- Thread sewing machine and bobbin with 50 weight 100% cotton thread.
- Attach an open-toe presser foot and select needle down if your machine has this option.
- Bring bobbin thread to the top of the fabric by lowering then raising the needle, bringing up the bobbin thread loop. Pull the loop all the way to the surface.
- Begin using a straight stitch and stitching 2 or 3 stitches in place (drop feed dogs or set stitch length at 0) or use your machine's lock stitch feature, if equipped to anchor thread.
- Switch the stitch setting to the selected Blanket Stitch.
- The vertical stitches should fall at the very outside edge of the appliqué piece with the horizontal stitches biting into the appliqué piece.
- When stitching outside curves (**Fig. 9**), stop with the needle down in the background fabric. Raise presser foot and pivot project as needed. Lower presser foot and continue stitching, pivoting as often as necessary to follow the curve.

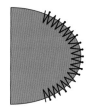

Fig. 9

- When stopping stitching, use a lock stitch to sew 2 or 3 stitches in place.

Quilting

Quilting holds the three layers (top, batting and backing) of the quilt together. Because marking, layering and quilting are interrelated and may be done in different orders depending on circumstances, please read entire Quilting section, pages 60 - 62, before beginning project.

PREPARING THE BACKING

To allow for slight shifting of quilt top during quilting, backing and batting should be 4" larger on all sides.

- Measure length and width of quilt top.
- If your finished quilt top is 79" or less in length, cut 2 lengths 8" longer than the width of your quilt top and piece your backing pieces together horizontally (**Fig. 10**).

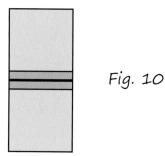

Fig. 10

- If your quilt top is longer than 79" and 79" or less in width, cut 2 lengths 8" longer than the length of your quilt and piece your backing pieces together vertically (**Fig. 11**).

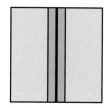

Fig. 11

- If your quilt top is longer than 79" and wider than 79", piece 3 lengths of fabric together either vertically or horizontally, whichever is the most economical use of fabric, remembering to add 8" to your horizontal or vertical cuts.

PILLOW BACKING

- All of the pillow backs are made with a two panel flap. The left panel sits over top the right panel and allows you to slip the pillow form in and out of the pillow cover for cleaning.

Pillows with Binding

- Fold and press ¼" of the left edge of the right panel to the back of the panel. Repeat then top stitch ⅛" in from the folded edge.
- With wrong sides together, line up the right edge of the right panel piece with the right edge of the pillow front. Pin in place.
- Fold the backing trim piece in half and press. Line up the raw edges of the trim with the right edge of the left panel piece (Fig. 12). Stitch together and then press the trim to the right over the stitching.
- Line up the left edge of the left panel piece with the left edge of the pillow front so the left panel pieces sits over top the right panel piece.

Fig. 12

- Use a scant ¼" seam to join the back panels to the pillow front.
- Prepare and attach binding to finish the pillow.

Pillows without Binding

- Finish the left edge of the right panel and the right edge of the left panel as for Pillows with Binding.
- With right sides together, line up the left edge of the left panel with the left edge of the pillow front and pin in place.
- Place the right panel over top of the left panel lining up the right edge of the right panel with the right edge of the pillow front and pin in place.
- Use a regular ¼" seam to join the front to the back. Turn the pillow right side out.

CHOOSING THE BATTING

- To achieve the look of the quilts in this book, choose a low-loft batting.
- Low-loft batting comes in cotton, cotton/polyester blend, all polyester, wool, silk or bamboo.
- Each of these products has different characteristics with respect to washing and shrinkage. Some are better for hand quilting and others are better for machine quilting.
- Read the manufacturer's label to choose a product that best suits your quilting method and your desired results.
- Cut batting to the same size as your backing.

ASSEMBLING THE QUILT

- Examine wrong side of quilt top closely; trim any threads that may show through front of the quilt. Press quilt top, being careful not to "set" any marked quilting lines.
- Place backing wrong side up on a flat surface. Use masking tape to tape edges of the backing to the surface. Place batting on top of backing fabric. Smooth batting gently, being careful not to stretch or tear it. Center quilt top right side up on batting.
- Use 1" rustproof safety pins to "pin-baste" all layers together, spacing pins approximately 4" apart. Begin at center and work toward outer edges to secure all layers. If possible, place pins away from areas that will be quilted, although pins may be removed as needed when quilting.
- Instead of pins, you can spray baste the layers together using a temporary basting spray like 505. After laying out the 3 layers as described above, fold back half the batting and half the quilt top from the center of the quilt and spray the wrong side of the backing. Fold the batting back, smoothing it out over the backing. Spray the batting, then fold the quilt top back, smoothing the quilt top over the batting. Repeat for other half of the quilt.

MACHINE QUILTING METHODS

Use general-purpose thread in bobbin. Do not use quilting thread. Thread the needle of machine with general-purpose thread or transparent mono filament thread to make quilting blend with quilt top fabrics Use decorative thread, such as a metallic or contrasting-color general-purpose thread, to make quilting lines stand out more.

Straight-Line Quilting

The term "straight line" is somewhat deceptive, since curves (especially gentle ones) as well as straight lines can be stitched with this technique.

- Set stitch length for six to ten stitches per inch and attach walking foot to sewing machine.
- Determine which section of quilt will have longest continuous quilting line, oftentimes area from center top to center bottom. Roll up and secure each edge of quilt to help reduce the bulk, keep fabrics smooth. Smaller projects may not need to be rolled.
- Begin stitching on longest quilting line, using very short stitches for the first ¼" to "lock" quilting. Stitch across project, using one hand on each side of walking foot to slightly spread fabric and to guide fabric through machine. Lock stitches at end of quilting line.
- Continue machine quilting, stitching longer quilting lines to stabilize quilt before moving on to other areas.

Free-Motion Quilting

Free-motion quilting may be free form or may follow a marked pattern.

- Attach a darning foot to sewing machine and lower or cover feed dogs.
- Position quilt under darning foot; lower foot. Holding top thread, take a stitch and pull bobbing thread to top of quilt. To "lock" beginning of quilting line, hold top and bobbin threads while making three to five stitches in place.
- Use one hand on each side of darning foot to slightly spread fabric and to move fabric through the machine. Even stitch length is achieved by using smooth, flowing hand motion and steady machine speed. Slow machine speed and fast hand movement will create long stitches. Fast machine speed and slow hand movement will create short stitches. Move quilt sideways, back and forth, in a circular motion, or in a random motion to create desired designs; do not rotate quilt. Lock stitches at end of each quilting line.

BINDING

Binding is used to enclose the raw edge of a quilt after the quilt top, batting and backing have been sewn together. Follow the binding instructions to bind both the quilt and pillow projects.

Making Binding

- With right sides together, and using diagonal seams (Fig. 13), sew the short ends of the binding strips together to make one continuous strip of binding.
- Fold the binding strip in half lengthwise.

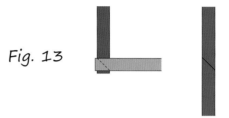

Fig. 13

Attaching Binding

- Beginning with one end near center on the bottom edge of the quilt, lay binding around the quilt to make sure that seams in binding will not end up at a corner. Adjust placement if necessary. Matching raw edges of binding to raw edge of quilt top, pin binding to right side of quilt along one edge.
- When you reach first corner, mark ¼" from corner of quilt top (Fig. 14).

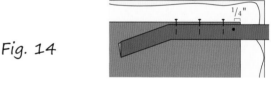

Fig. 14

- Beginning approximately 10" from end of binding and using ¼" seam allowance, sew binding to quilt, back stitching at beginning of stitching and at mark (Fig. 15). Lift needle out of fabric and clip thread.

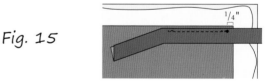

Fig. 15

- Fold binding as shown in Figs. 16-17 and pin binding to adjacent side, matching raw edges. When you've reached the next corner, mark ¼" from edge of quilt top.

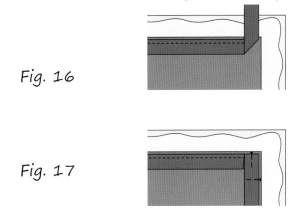

Fig. 16

Fig. 17

- Back stitching at edge of quilt top, sew pinned binding to quilt (Fig. 18); back stitch at the next mark. Lift needle out of fabric and clip thread.

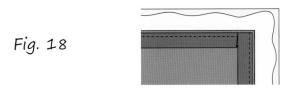

Fig. 18

- Continue sewing binding to quilt, stopping approximately 10" from starting point (Fig. 19).

Fig. 19

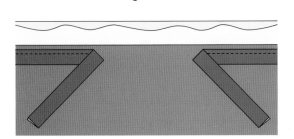

- Bring beginning and end of binding to center of opening and fold each end back, leaving a ¼" space between folds (Fig. 20). Finger press folds.

Fig. 20

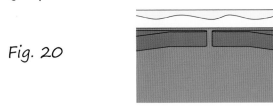

- Unfold ends of binding and draw a line across wrong side in finger-pressed crease. Draw a line through the lengthwise pressed fold of binding at the same spot to create a cross mark. With edge of ruler at cross mark, line up 45° angle marking on ruler with one long side of binding. Draw a diagonal line from edge to edge. Repeat on remaining end, making sure that the two diagonal lines are angled the same way (Fig. 21).

Fig. 21

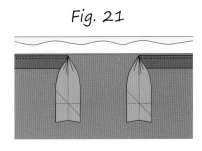

- Matching right sides and diagonal lines, pin binding ends together at right angles (Fig. 22).

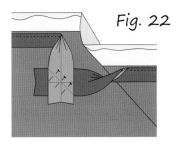

Fig. 22

- Machine stitch along diagonal line (Fig. 23), removing pins as you stitch.

Fig. 23

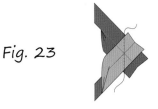

- Lay binding against quilt to double check that it is correct length.
- Trim binding ends, leaving ¼" seam allowance; press seam open. Stitch binding to quilt.
- Trim backing and batting even with edges

of quilt top.

- On one edge of quilt, fold binding over to quilt backing and pin pressed edge in place, covering stitching line (Fig. 24). On adjacent side, fold binding over, forming a mitered corner (Fig. 25). Repeat to pin remainder of binding in place.

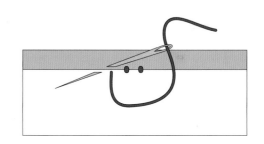

Fig. 26

Fig. 24   Fig. 25

- Blind stitch binding to backing, taking care not to stitch through to front of quilt.

Blind Stitch
Come up at 1, go down at 2, and come up at 3 (Fig. 26). Length of stitches may be varied as desired.

SIGNING AND DATING YOUR QUILT
A completed quilt is a work of art and should be signed and dated. There are many different ways to do this and numerous books on the subject. The label should reflect the style of the quilt, the occasion or person for which it was made, and the quilter's own particular talents.

Metric Conversion Chart	
Inches x 2.54 = centimeters (cm)	Yards x .9144 = meters (m)
Inches x 25.4 = millimeters (mm)	Yards x 91.44 = centimeters (cm)
Inches x .0254 = meters (m)	Centimeters x .3937 = inches (")
	Meters x 1.0936 = yards (yd)

Standard Equivalents					
1/8"	3.2 mm	0.32 cm	1/8 yard	11.43 cm	0.11 m
1/4"	6.35 mm	0.635 cm	1/4 yard	22.86 cm	0.23 m
3/8"	9.5 mm	0.95 cm	3/8 yard	34.29 cm	0.34 m
1/2"	12.7 mm	1.27 cm	1/2 yard	45.72 cm	0.46 m
5/8"	15.9 mm	1.59 cm	5/8 yard	57.15 cm	0.57 m
3/4"	19.1 mm	1.91 cm	3/4 yard	68.58 cm	0.69 m
7/8"	22.2 mm	2.22 cm	7/8 yard	80 cm	0.8 m
1"	25.4 mm	2.54 cm	1 yard	91.44 cm	0.91 m